Critiquing Moral Arguments

Robert G. Pielke, Ph.D.
Claremont Graduate School

Philosophy Department
El Camino College
Torrance, California

UNIVERSITY
PRESS OF
AMERICA

Lanham • New York • London

Copyright © 1992 by
University Press of America®, Inc.
4720 Boston Way
Lanham, Maryland 20706

3 Henrietta Street
London WC2E 8LU England

Library of Congress Cataloging-in-Publication Data

Pielke, Robert G., 1942–
Critiquing moral arguments / by Robert G. Pielke.
p.   cm.
Includes bibliographical references and index.
1. Ethics.   2. Judgment (Ethics).   I. Title.
BJ1012.P54   1992   170'.42—dc20   92–7955 CIP

ISBN 0–8191–8642–2 (cloth : alk. paper)
ISBN 0–8191–8643–0 (pbk. : alk. paper)

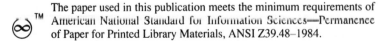

The paper used in this publication meets the minimum requirements of
American National Standard for Information Sciences—Permanence
of Paper for Printed Library Materials, ANSI Z39.48–1984.

**for Emily,
whenever I may find her**

CONTENTS

INTRODUCTION

In a complex world that is undergoing changes as momentous as they are unpredictable, it is more likely than not that we will eventually become embroiled in arguments involving drastically differing opinions. With abortion, euthanasia, flag burning, sex, pollution, homelessness, drugs, racism, war and free expression occupying so much of our collective attention, at the very least we will be forced to witness the arguments of others — in the media, if not in our immediate presence.

So what do we do about this? These arguments are not just academic debates, after all; they manifest some of our deepest feelings about life and existence. As such, they are not to be trifled with. Disagreements over such convictions are never pleasant, and can even lead to violence, especially when the conflict is not dealt with wisely. This does not mean, however, that it is always inappropriate to voice our disagreement. In fact, there are times when disagreements must be voiced in the strongest possible terms. While there is a time and place for such disputes, most of us would probably prefer to keep these times and places to a minimum.

Short of a violent confrontation, there are a variety of forms in which disagreements can take place. The moods can vary from friendly to antagonistic. The goals can include seeking a simple clarification, aiming for a resolution, settling for a compromise or maybe even hoping for a conversion. All of them seem quite legitimate depending on the circumstances, but no matter what form it might take, a disagreement over fundamental moral convictions must inevitably involve a critique.

In the chapters that follow, I will clarify exactly what does and does not characterize a legitimate critique, and offer some suggestions on how to proceed. The examples provided herein will be exclusively of the moral kind. Afterwards, it should be apparent that these same critical procedures can be of use in evaluating any kind of argument.

Assistance in completing this book has come from many persons and in many ways. First, there are my students throught the years who have challenged my ideas in and out of class. I have learned much more about the process of critiquing from them than they will ever know. Second, there are my friends and family members who, often indirectly, encouraged me — especially my daughter, Karen. Finally, no book can succeed without editorial assistance. In this respect, Clint Bradford has been invaluable.

Chapter One

CRITIQUING *VS.* CRITICIZING

Everyone can remember being told at one time or another not to criticize. It wasn't polite. It might even have been morally offensive. At the time, under certain circumstances, this admonition may well have been wholly justified. Yet its proper use on such occasions has more often than not destroyed the desirability of being critical on other occasions.

It is frequently not recognized that the word "criticize" is ambiguous. It has two completely distinct meanings — each one having an appropriate manifestation in a given context, but misleading, unintelligible, or even offensive if manifested in the wrong situation. On the one hand, "to criticize" can mean "to condemn," "to find fault with," or "to blame." When used correctly, for defensible reasons, there is absolutely nothing wrong with such "criticism." On the other hand, "to criticize" can also mean "to consider the merits and demerits," "to assess the worth of an idea," or simply "to evaluate." Given the proper context, "criticism" in this sense can also be unproblematically utilized. Problems arise when the differences between the two are not recognized.

Consider some of the implications that follow from these two contrary meanings. First, the objects of "criticism" are most likely to be quite different. In the first, condemnatory sense, the attack is usually directed towards a person or group of persons; whereas in the second, analytical sense, an argument or an idea is attacked.

This highlights a second implication, namely, a difference in attitude. In the first case, the attack can not avoid being personal, and potentially volatile as a consequence. Finding a person's character blameworthy will almost certainly raise the emotional level of any disagreement. In the second case, the attack has a far better chance of being dispassionate. The attack will, of course, have as its ultimate target a

2

person's cherished moral beliefs, yet the object under scrutiny is still that which is under consideration and not the person doing the consideration. Finally, the effectiveness or worth the "criticism," will depend, in the first sense, on the attacker being in some way "superior" to the person or persons under attack. It would do no good, according to the old aphorism, for the "pot to call the kettle black." The criteria for success, in other words, are wholly dependent on whoever is making the criticism. They are more than subjective — they are arbitrary. In the second sense, the attacker's own position and argument is irrelevant, as is his or her character. The only thing that matters is the value of the attack itself. The criteria for success are completely independent of the attacker. They are objective. To put it even more succinctly, the merits of a credible "criticism" are, in the first case, in the attacker, while in the second, they are in the attack.

Obviously, the intention of this book is to discuss the nature of "criticism" in the second sense. Because of this ambiguity, however, it might be more helpful to restrict what I am doing to the word, "critique." In so doing, I think the meaning of the second, analytic, sense is captured fully without any lingering traces of the first. So as to avoid any subtle or not so subtle confusion, the term "critique" will be used henceforth in this book.

Perhaps the proceeding will help in clarifying yet another typical confusion in making a critique. It is often assumed that such an attack can only legitimately concern itself with beliefs a person finds morally objectionable. This, however, is to misunderstand the nature of a critique. A critique, properly understood, is always focused on the premises of an argument — not on the conclusion they are intended to support. It is both logically and psychologically possible to consider the virtues as well as the vices of an argument in complete independence of the conclusion. Properly speaking, however, a critique will give paramount, if not exclusive attention to its vices. Attending to its virtues, or praising it, is to play the role of an advocate — not a critic. The two roles are not at all compatible.

It should be kept in mind that it is entirely possible for an argument to be severely critiqued by a person who nevertheless fervently agrees with the conclusion. Likewise, a person who just as fervently disagrees with the conclusions might find much to praise about the argument. The intentions of the persons making two such critiques would obviously differ, but intentions are irrelevant both as a criterion for defining the parameters of a critique as well as for assessing its worth. In the first instance, the intention would be to provide better support for the conclusion; whereas in the

Robert G. Pielke

second, the intention would be to demolish it. Nevertheless, they are both legitimate approaches to doing a critique.

As an illustration of the former, both Mary Anne Warren and Jane English are ardent advocates of a woman's right to choose an abortion.[1] Yet English finds Warren's attempts to define humanity inherently impossible, and tries to reduce Warren's definitional criteria to absurdity. She then provides what she believes is a superior defense for their pro-choice position. As an illustration of the latter, Peter Singer and Garrett Hardin differ dramatically concerning the international distribution of scarce resources.[2] Singer feels that affluent societies have a moral obligation to assist the needy as long as nothing of moral significance is sacrificed in the process. Hardin feels that all such attempts would be naive and certainly counter-productive. Despite their very real differences, both are reasoning from virtually the same utilitarian perspective, and both have surprisingly similar values. Both, for example, find starvation *per se* abhorrent; they would prefer that everyone have enough to eat. Their differences concern essentially factual matters.

Finally, there is often an admonition confronted by those making a critique: "If you can't say anything positive (or nice?), don't say anything at all!" If this phrase has any clear meaning at all, it can only have to do with admonishing people not to "criticize" (or blame) others in the sense used earlier. While this might indeed be a virtue for some, it is for most a matter of taste, or etiquette. As such it does not concern us here. Both "criticizing" and "critiquing" have an appropriate use, although determining when and where this might be the case will often present considerably difficulties. Not infrequently, neither is appropriate.

There is another sense in which some critiques might be said to be positive and others negative. It involves the fact that critiques are intrinsically evaluative. A positive evaluation would be one that concludes that there are more merits than flaws to an argument. A negative evaluation would be one that concludes the reverse. In such instances, both positive and negative critiques are not only not inappropriate, they are the very essence of a critique. It should always be remembered, however, that conclusions of this kind are never simply a matter of weighing the pluses and minuses. A good critique must always assess the relative worth of pluses and minuses. The critical process is far more qualitative than it is quantitative. When D. H. M. Brooks attacks Michael Levin's opposition to anti-discriminatory programs based on Affirmative Action, he does so by focusing on only one component of Levin's argument.[3] This component is by far the key element as far as Brooks is concerned — Levin's allegation that racial discrimination is not a collective wrong but the violation of an individual. On the other hand, Gregory Kavka cites many factors in disputing Douglas Lackey's advocacy of unilateral nuclear disarmament.[4] Seemingly, he feels that a preponderance of critical points is necessary — no one or two being sufficient to do the job. In both of these cases, of course, it is incumbent on the person conducting the critique to provide a rationale for the relative importance of the factors selected for scrutiny. This is rarely a simple task, but it is often the cornerstone of a successful critique.

Overall, a critique of a moral argument (or of any other kind of argument for that matter) is a question of attitude, the philosophical attitude. Although difficult to capture in terms of a typical definition, it has to do with wonder, curiosity, uncertainty, doubt and the never-ending process of questioning. Everything, including especially one's most cherished positions, should, in keeping with the philosophical attitude, be constantly suspect and subject to revision or possible abandonment. For a legitimate critique can not be accomplished without the willingness to undergo the very same kind of scrutiny the critic has in mind for others.

This, then, is what it means to critique a moral argument. It should be recognized that these conditions are goals and not prerequisites. All genuine critiques strive to meet them, but most critiques fall short in one way or another. Yet as long as a sincere attempt is being made, it is entirely proper to think of it as a more or less legitimate critique. After considering the ideas expressed in the remainder of the book, it should be easier to come significantly closer to the "more" side of the continuum. It should also be easier to approach more closely a successful critique.

Chapter Two

THE ELEMENTS OF A MORAL ARGUMENT

Moral arguments, like all forms of argumentation, are intended to persuade — to convince an audience of something debatable. They are unique in that they try to support the contention that an action is right, wrong, or obligatory — or a related contention that some character trait is either desirable or undesirable. What makes the intended goal moral, rather than merely aesthetic or prudential, is its relevance for the prevention of harm and its universalizability. What distinguishes it from a legal contention is the absence of any institutionalized mechanism for its origin and sanction. And, most important, what differentiates it from a factual assertion is its being prescriptive rather than descriptive.

Given these general features, there are several crucial elements that comprise any argument intended to support a moral conclusion. Some might be more prominent than others in any given case, but all are necessary components.

Factual Data

Whether evident or not, there are no moral arguments that do not in some way rely on a foundation of factual material. This should not be misconstrued as moral arguments having to rely on verified or unquestionable data. Empirical certainty is unlikely in any kind of argument. Factual assertions can be true only within greater or lesser degrees of probability. The crucial questions in a moral argument concern the relevance and scope of the factual claims relied on.

Usually, much of this material can be quite fairly assumed to be within the realm of common knowledge. Arguments concerning abortion, for example, must take into account such things as the nature of fetal development from conception to birth, the history of abortion legislation,

6

Critiquing Moral Arguments

the social consequences of both legalization and prohibition, and the overall political environment. None of this, of course, will alone support a moral conclusion, but no argument relating to abortion can proceed in a factual vacuum.

Moral Principles

Although certainly an obvious component, it needs to be pointed out that such principles are quite varied. Some are general, others are quire specific, and still others serve to mediate between the two. Determining which are appropriate depends largely on the context of the argument. Controversies over deterrence as a nuclear strategy, for example, need not appeal to the general principle of war being undesirable — this is rarely, if ever, a matter of rational dispute. More likely is a dispute concerning intermediate principles, those relating to how we should go about preventing war in general and nuclear wars in particular.

Further, if the argument is classical in nature, the principles will pertain to character; while modern arguments will emphasize behavior. This should be recognized in any effective critique. Attacking a classicist for not focusing on behavior (or a contemporary ethicist foe de-emphasizing the role of character traits) would not only be beside the point, it would betray a fundamental and inexcusable ignorance about the nature of moral reasoning. In effect, an attack of this nature would amount to accusing someone of doing exactly what he or she claims to be doing!

Moral Reasoning

No matter what content a moral argument has, it will be structured in terms of either teleological or deontological reasoning, or some combination of the two. Each one has its characteristic strengths and weaknesses, and these must be understood for a critique to have even the possibility of being effective. Without taking this factor into account, it is no exaggeration to say that a critique will always miss its mark.

To attack Kant for not taking into account the overall balance of good and evil, when arguing for the exceptionless obligation to keep promises, would be absurd. Similarly, to accuse Jeremy Bentham of ignoring the intrinsic differences in value between different kinds of pleasures would be to exhibit gross ignorance about his thinking process.

Robert G. Pielke

Justification

Normative arguments hardly ever make this dimension of moral thinking explicit. Nevertheless, it is an inescapable facet of all moral reasoning. Everyone has some position on whether or not moral judgments can be justified. Whether stated or unstated, however, it never affects the quality of the reasoning in any way. It might, in rare cases, affect how fervently a conviction is held. If so, this would only be of psychological — not philosophical — interest. It is often assumed (erroneously) that to claim truth for one's basic moral principles is in some way an indicator of the intrinsic quality of an argument. Absolutists, those who believe that a rational justification is possible, are, accordingly, assumed to have a fundamentally stronger case than relativists, those who deny that a justification is even intelligible. This would come as a surprise to such adamant relativists as Bertrand Russell and H. L. A. Hart, whose convictions are supported with as much skill and ardor as any of their absolutist opponents.

Concepts

Conceptual distinctions are the tools of philosophical thinking, and as such they need to be maintained in excellent working condition. Refinement, sharpening and modification in the light of continual scrutiny are the relevant procedures for doing so. Most important, they should not call unnecessary attention to themselves, thus making themselves the bones of contention. If this happens, the conceptual tools become virtually useless. Both John Rawls and Robert Nozick are able to carry on and engender an extensive and productive debate precisely because they succeeded in clarifying such concepts as "liberal," "anarchy," "state," "veil of ignorance," and the like. To illustrate what happens when no clarity or agreement exists, consider the arguments surrounding "free will" and "determinism." The former has never acquired any consistent meaning, and the latter is variously, and confusingly, subdivided into "hard" and "soft" versions. In both cases, almost every ethicist wishing to make use of these terms has to spend a considerable amount of time stipulating how they are to be utilized — or prescribing how they "ought" to be utilized.

Critiquing Moral Arguments

Cases

In general, there are two ways in which moral arguments make use of cases (both actual and hypothetical). First, they might be cited as integral parts of the argument, becoming premises in effect. More often than not, this approach takes the form of inductive reasoning, where an accumulation of past moral judgments, deemed to be relevantly similar to a current problem, results in a more or less confident moral judgment. This is best exemplified by the casuistries of Roman Catholic morality, Orthodox Judaism and the common law tradition in both England and the United States. The U. S. Supreme Court decision in the case of *U. C. Regents v. Allan Bakke*, to cite a recent controversial example, refers to a whole series of prior cases as direct support. In a very real sense, the past is invested with moral authority and made the basis of a prescriptive appeal. Often, the more ancient the tradition, the more authoritative the basis it is considered to be.

Second, cases might be cited as illustrations or examples only. John Stuart Mill, in his famous essay "On Liberty," first explains and defends the "harm principle," wherein the state is only justified in interfering with an individual's action when it threatens the possibility of harm to others. Only then does he provide illustrations. His argument is entirely independent of the relevance or, indeed, even the intelligibility of the cases he cites. Their purpose is to provide clarity — not rational support.

It should be added that it is by no means always easy to identify how cases are being used. Furthermore, it is not impossible that a case might serve both functions.

Analogies

Like the use of case studies, analogies (both actual and hypothetical) can be used in basically two ways: as direct support and as illustrations. Religious ethicists often call to mind stories about various sacred personalities in order to provide authoritative guidelines (or rules) for contemporary living. These stories and persons are then invested with moral authority, becoming in the process moral guidelines. Their putative similarities with situations today provide the essential linkage in the overall argument.

Robert G. Pielke

Alternatively, used as illustrative material, analogies function to clarify a person's point of view. As with the parallel use of cases, they are completely independent of the argument, and provide no rational support whatsoever.

The Conclusion

Obviously, the conclusion of a moral argument is a moral judgment of some sort. This, in fact, is what distinguishes a moral argument from other kinds. It is important to recognize, however, that such conclusions may vary in specificity from a judgment intended for one particular instance to the most abstract of general principles — and the reasoning must vary accordingly.

Kant's application of his "categorical imperative" yielded only the most general guidance, e.g., the strict obligations to keep promises and tell the truth. Adam Smith's version of Ethical Egoism resulted in more specific guidance, e.g., the admonition that being charitable is often in one's own best interest, and is hence prudential. Still more specific is James Madison's plea (along with the other writers of the "Federalist Papers") that the proposed Constitution for the United States be ratified by the thirteen newly created states. Continuing with increasing specificity, politicians are in the business of urging the public to vote for them. Most specific of all, however, are the moral judgments that recommend not only a particular course of action, but recommend this to a particular person.

Sometimes, for rhetorical purposes, the conclusion will be left unstated. At other times, for more nefarious purposes or out of ignorance on the part of the person making the argument, the conclusion is disguised. In all such cases, it is incumbent on the critic to identify clearly what is suppressed.

Chapter Three

HOW NOT TO PROCEED

In addition to the tendency to criticize mentioned in the first chapter, there are at least five major kinds of mistakes often made in the attempt to critique a moral argument. All of them result from losing sight of what constitutes a moral argument in the first place.

Focusing on the Conclusion

It is tempting to zero in on the whole purpose of the argument, the disputed judgment itself. After all, why not "go for the jugular"? Why waste time puttering about with incidentals?

The reason, of course, is that the conclusion is <u>not</u> the jugular — and the reasoning process is <u>not</u> incidental. To analogize critiquing an argument with killing an animal is far more serious an error than it might seem at first. Not only are there no similarities of any kind between an argument and animal, there are also no similarities between critiquing and killing. Animals are organisms that have as their only discernible purpose self-preservation or self-fulfillment; while arguments exist solely for purposes set for them <u>by</u> organisms — in order to achieve preservation or fulfillment for the self, or selves. In other words, animals are ends in themselves, while arguments are means only. Further, to critique is inherently positive; it provides the person making an argument with the means for improvement — even if this is not in any way the motivation for the critique. To kill, on the other hand, is inherently negative; regardless of the motivation, the result is destruction.

Using the faulty analogy as the implicit support for a concentration of the conclusion, it should be obvious why such an effort is bound to fail. It can not destroy anything; and it can not offer an opportunity for improvement. The alleged critique winds up being nothing other than the

12

Critiquing Moral Arguments

expression of a different opinion. To maintain, for example, that women should have the right to choose for themselves whether or not to have an abortion is not a critique of the notion that a fetus has an absolute right to life. Since the argument itself is ignored, so also may this kind of attack.

Disagreeing with Moral Principles

If reasons should ever be given as to why the conclusion should be rejected, a second temptation is to center an attack on the supporting moral principles. The conclusion, after all, is a moral judgment, so why should its props not be kicked out from under it if possible? At the very least, it would seem to be obvious that they should be challenged.

The idea behind this tactic is perfectly appropriate — to direct an attack against the support given for the conclusion. The problem is that merely disagreeing with any of the supporting moral principles will not do this. On the contrary, to disagree with them is often to grant them a degree of legitimacy that they might not otherwise have. Disagreement amounts to stating an alternative, but this in turn presupposes an idea sufficiently clear and persuasive to allow for, and even demand, a response. In a way, the more strenuous the disagreement, the greater the acknowledgment of legitimacy. Poorly expressed and/or patently absurd moral principles occasion little comment, let alone the effort required to disagree.

If disagreement is nevertheless expressed, logically, an alternative set of supporting reasons must be supplied. This, however, is not a critique of the original. The alternative could just as well be presented had the original never been presented in the first place. To continue with the abortion issue, one of the moral convictions typically used to support the "pro-life" (or "anti-choice") position is the claim that biological humanity ought to be regarded as sufficient for determining the right to life. Merely to disagree, and maintain instead that the acquisition of self-awareness (for example) should be both necessary and sufficient, it completely beside the point.

Editorializing

To editorialize is to do more than express and defend an alternative moral judgment. It is to opine on its virtues as opposed to that which is being rejected. Seemingly this does constitute a genuine critique. It not only acknowledges the original position, it seeks to point out its alleged vices.

The intention is to proclaim how immoral it would be to accept the original conclusion, and by extension to accuse anyone who does so is immoral. It does not, however, constitute a legitimate critique. On the contrary, it is either a thinly disguised disagreement or simply begging the question. To assert the virtues of one moral position over another does entail more than the assertion itself. It involves a reasoned defense as to why it is morally superior, and this boils down to mere disagreement. Clearly, the proponents of the original position would feel exactly the same about the judgment they are asserting, and would provide their own reasoned defense. This may seem like more than a disagreement, but it is only a more elaborate way of asserting a moral position. Furthermore, to proclaim any moral judgment to be morally superior to its rivals is conceptionally identical to the mere proclamation of the judgment by itself. To say that it is superior to all the alternatives adds nothing. Why else would it be asserted in the first place? The supporters of the "pro-choice" (or "pro-abortion") position do nothing to critique their opponents by castigating them as "anti-choice," proclaiming "choice" to be morally superior to the preservation of the fetus' life — no matter how extensively its superiority is supported.

Preoccupation with Facts

If anything is relevant to a genuine critique, questioning the factual support would seem to be one of the top contenders. It is certainly true that moral judgments will be mistaken or incorrectly applied when the empirical beliefs on which they rest are incorrect; however, it would never be immoral to act in accordance with such judgments. Unless people are lying (which is another issue entirely), they do believe the factual claims that support their moral judgments to be true. To be shown that this is not the case would probably require the retraction or at the very least a modification of their judgment — but it would not, by itself, require the abandonment of any of their moral convictions.

Advocates of "pro-choice" might find that "pro-lifers" erroneously believe that the prohibition of legal abortions would lead to more adoptions. To contend that this is an error is not to critique their argument that abortions (with the possibility of one or more exceptions) are morally wrong. Nor is it a critique to point out that a fetus' response to stimuli is not axiomatically an indication of sentience. "Pro-lifers" would properly regard such information, correct or not, to be beside the point.

Critiquing Moral Arguments

Misdirection into Justification

It might seem that to admit that a fervently held moral conviction has no truth value whatsoever would irreparably weaken it. Conversely, it might seem fatal to attempt a truth claim on behalf of a moral judgment and have it demolished. Actually, neither is the case.

It is an interesting question as to whether or not moral judgments have any cognitive status, and if they do, to what extent their status can be known. It is, nevertheless, quite consistent to assert an action to be right, wrong, or obligatory while at the same time denying that these assertions can be true or false. It is equally consistent to maintain the truth of a moral conviction while admitting that the truth of this contention can never be shown to anyone who does not already believe it. Moral judgments involve a pro or con attitude toward a person's action or character, while questions of justification have to do with the theory of language.

"Pro-life" advocates often appeal to the idea that moral judgments are completely translatable into assertions of metaphysical, theological, or natural facts. To argue that this makes no logical sense is not in any way to dispute their judgment that abortions are wrong. Abortions might still be wrong even though "pro-lifers" might not be able to "prove" it. A critique of moral reasoning at one level (in this instance, the metaethical level) is in no way a critique at another (in this instance, the normative).

Critiquing a "Critique"

It is worth noting that citing any of these fallacious attempts to critique an argument is itself a critique. While such a "meta-critique" might seem to be beside the point any maybe even a little arch, it is not. For to allow a pseudo-critique to pass as the real thing is now, always has been, and always will be philosophically inexcusable.

Chapter Four

THE CRITIQUE

It is unlikely that any moral argument will fall prey to more than a few of the following critical points. Nevertheless, they should all be considered during the evaluative process. It should be remembered that the quantity of critical points is not significant; their quality is all that matters. To point out one serious flaw in an argument is far more devastating than to make a multitude of minor criticisms. (An argument with many serious flaws is hardly worth critiquing anyway, and it would almost certainly not be published — almost.)

It should also be remembered that finding a flaw is only the beginning. The critic must then show why it is a flaw and indicate how the overall argument is adversely affected. Failure to follow through on these latter two objectives is, more often than not, the reason why a promising critique misses its mark.

The Philisophical Attitude

Although its presence is difficult to detect, a willingness to question everything — including especially one's most deeply held beliefs — is of paramount significance. This is the only genuine safeguard against a critique degenerating into mere personal criticism. A helpful tactic is to speculate consciously how to go about critiquing one's own position on the topic in question — and to do so as if it were being done by one's most savage opponent. This need not imply, however, that a critique must be dispassionate, devoid of emotion and conviction. Far from it! It only means that strong feelings must not be allowed to interfere with the critique. No matter how fervently and vociferously a critique is conducted, these emotions neither add nor detract from the quality or the success of the criticism.

Critiquing Moral Arguments

Clarity & Precision

One of the most common failings in any kind of argument is lack of clarity and precision. Sometimes this is done deliberately in order to avoid making specific claims — thus presenting nothing specific to attack. This belief is mistaken, of course, since this very implication, itself, provides an ample target.

In one of the most controversial articles of recent years, Albert Carr argues that truth telling is not a moral requirement in business relationships as it is in ordinary personal relationships.[5] Rather, the former should be looked at as "games." This being the case, what might rightfully be understood as a lie between individuals should be seen as "bluffing" within the business world.

The success of his argument depends not only on how well he can construct the analogy between games (in this case Poker) and business, but also on the imprecision of the two key terms, "games" and "bluffing." Neither is carefully defined at any place in the article, but the impression is created that they are. At one point, Carr refers to "bluffing" as "some kind of deception" — a claim that obviously begs for a further analysis. This could quite legitimately mean "deceiving" the Jehovah's Witnesses at your door by pretending not to be at home when they ring the bell. It could also mean cooking with ground turkey instead of ground beef in order to lower your family's cholesterol. It would certainly include telling your children the story of Santa Claus, as well as convincing the homicidal maniac at your door that your friend who is, in fact, hiding in your house has long since departed.

"Game" fares no better in the article. Apart from the implicit suggestion that, whatever they are, they are all like Poker, Carr merely describes a "game" as something that has "special" rules and requires a "special strategy." So does dating! It is hard to think of something that doesn't!

As far as a critique of the argument is concerned, however, it takes more than to point out the vague ideas. It must be shown exactly how this vagueness affects the argument, how it prevents the conclusion from following from the premises. In this case, Carr's conclusion depends on "bluffing" and "game" having very specific meanings — those which he does not provide. A "bluff" must not be life-threatening and always recognized as a possibility. Otherwise, it could not possibly be morally

Robert G. Pielke

acceptable in any context. A "game" must be of indeterminate length and include the possibility that more than the announced players are involved. Obviously, with such elements included implicitly in the definitions, his argument can not possibly succeed. "Bluffing" would indeed be included within "ordinary morality," and "game" would be an absurdity.

The same kind of flaw is evident in many articles about "pornography." It is unfair to expect agreement on the meaning of this term, and it is equally unfair to expect everyone with an opinion on the subject to present and defend a definition. Nevertheless, it is not too much to ask for them to stipulate how they intend to use the term. G. L. Simons, for example, raises the question "Is Pornography Beneficial?" then proceeds to argue that in many ways it is.[6] Obviously, something must be said about the meaning of pornography if this claim is to have any hope of serious consideration. Yet the reader is left only with the merest of clues as to what he has in mind. "Certain types of sexual material" is about as specific as he gets.

A critique of his argument would entail suggesting how some examples of pornography might indeed be conceived of as beneficial, while other examples might just as easily be conceived of as harmful. The point of citing such examples is not to contend with the conclusion — all forms of pornography might be as beneficial as Simons claims — but to point out that this conclusion can not possibly follow without first clarifying exactly what is meant by "pornography."

It is not always apparent in an argument which terms lack the requisite clarity. After all, it must be assumed that both writer and reader share a common language, and that it is not necessary to define everything. The critic must be sensitive to which terms are both unclear and crucial for the argument to proceed, and there is simply no infallible way to determine when this is the case.

Conceptual Vagueness

Every moral argument must make use of certain conceptual tools peculiar to the issue under discussion. Of necessity, these tools must be finely honed if they are to perform their specific tasks.

When dealing with the issue of Affirmative Action (or Reverse Discrimination), for example, the conceptual dilemmas surrounding "collective responsibility" must be dealt with. While it makes perfect sense to attribute moral responsibility to gangs, cabals, and possibly corporations, it remains to be seen whether the attribution of praise, blame, punishments, and rewards to racial, ethnic, and sex groups can be similarly understood. It is not incumbent on either proponents or opponents of this latter attribution to persuade their readers to accept their respective positions; this would amount to an impossible criterion. On the other hand, it is incumbent on them both to make their positions clear.

A notorious failure in this respect is evident in the majority opinion in *University of California v. Bakke* written by Justice Lewis F. Powell, Jr.[7] After reducing to absurdity the notion that a set number of places be set aside for members of certain groups ("quotas"), Powell goes on to argue that the admissions programs of universities may take race into account in order to achieve educational diversity. This both denies and acknowledges a person's race as an attribute deserving of distributive consideration. The inevitable result is confusion, evidenced by the amount of litigation occasioned by the numerous Affirmative Action programs following this decision.

Another problematic concept comes into play when considering euthanasia. Although admittedly difficult to utilize in many cases, the distinction between "active" and "passive" euthanasia is crucial. The American Medical Association, for example, forbids the former but permits the latter — judgments still echoed in the legislation of most states. J. Gay-Williams lays out three independent arguments in defense of this distinction and the traditional moral assessments proclaimed by the AMA.[8] In so doing, he never sufficiently clarifies exactly how he is using these terms. His only clue is to distinguish them in terms of intentions — "active" euthanasia intends the death of the patient, while "passive" euthanasia intends something more desirable. Obviously, if the morality of an action is to be determined by the agent's intentions, it is possible for the very same act to be both right and wrong — a logically very unsatisfactory situation.

A similar distinction exists whenever "rights" are at issue. While it may be similarly difficult to apply, there is a fundamental and significant difference between "positive" and "negative" rights. The former impose duties on others to assist in the fulfillment of the right, and the latter impose duties merely not to interfere. Thomas E. Hill, Jr., in an article often anthologized, "Servility and Self-Respect," is at pains to explain why servility is a moral flaw.[9] He can only come to what he freely admits is a very "limited" conclusion, which never successfully draws a line between servility and self-sacrifice. It would be different, he adds, if it could be assumed that some rights cannot be waived no matter what a person desires. Attributing certain positive rights to the self would enable him to do so. Not once does he make use of the two notions of rights. Had he done so, it might have enabled him to say that being servile is wrong, because it necessarily involves a violation of a positive right to self-respect. So conceived, others would have a duty never to treat anyone with servility — this, regardless of what a person in his or her ignorance might want. Instead, Hill struggles to find a path that avoids triviality on the one hand and absurdity on the other. (Omissions as well as commissions are fair game for critical scrutiny.)

A final example concerns the seemingly unproblematic notion of supererogatory actions, actions above and beyond the call of duty or self-sacrificial acts. Peter Singer, in his article "Famine, Affluence and Morality," argues that the Needy are owed as much assistance as possible as long as nothing of moral significance is sacrificed in the process. Unlike many persons who might make such a claim, he is fully aware that this upsets the traditional ways that moral categories are used. For that which is a person's duty can not at the same time be above and beyond the call of duty. Yet while he acknowledges this anomaly, he fails to make sense of it. He wants both to abolish the distinction as well as maintain it. This is not logically — or morally — possible.

A similar, but even more flawed, usage of this term is evident in Bertram and Elsie Bandman's attempt to draw a line between justifiable and unjustifiable acts of euthanasia.[10] They merely contend that sometimes it is our duty to risk our lives for others, apparently oblivious to the conceptual confusion thus created

The Role of Logic

Critiquing moral arguments does not presuppose being familiar with the principles of formal or informal logic, but it does entail having a sensitivity for their underlying rationale. One of the basic characteristics of a valid argument, for example, is the fact that the conclusion must necessarily follow, and that its contrary or contradictory can not. If it can be shown that the latter is the case, the critic has successfully pointed out a structural flaw.

For a variety of reasons (ambiguity of words, phrases, and concepts not being the least of them), many arguments, moral and otherwise, are suspect in this regard. Returning to one of J. Gay-Williams' arguments against euthanasia, he wants to maintain that valuing human dignity implies

Critiquing Moral Arguments

respect for the survival instinct and thus a prohibition of active euthanasia. Yet it could just as easily be maintained, and this would have to be demonstrated by a critic, that valuing human dignity implies the permissibility of active euthanasia. (It should be noted, of course, that active euthanasia still might be morally wrong — but not for the reason cited.)

Another fundamental tenet of logic is the principle that key phrases, terms, and concepts must be used consistently throughout the entire argument. To shift meanings in process is to equivocate. Often, the shift is subtle — an obvious shift of meaning is usually easy to detect and hence to correct or perhaps conceal. No matter how subtle, however, equivocation is a serious problem.

In one of Lisa Newton's otherwise provocative articles, "Reverse Discrimination As Unjustified," her contention is that no sense can be made of the claim that a group's rights have been violated, unless the group was first legally entitled to that which was denied.[11] Her point is well taken, but only if her argument uses the concept of "rights" consistently — but she doesn't. She begins with an analysis of the moral criteria involved with the distribution of rights, then moves to a consideration of how Affirmative Action programs seek to grant compensation for the violation of non-existent legal rights. It is always possible to ascribe moral rights to an individual or a group not currently recognized in the law — a possibility obviated by her equivocation.

Another fatal defect in reasoning is to presuppose, in one of many possible ways, the very idea expressed by the conclusion. Variously called "begging the question" or "circular reasoning," the reasons cited as support for the conclusion are actually no different from the conclusion itself. It thus makes it intrinsically impossible for each premise to be true or false independent of the conclusion, a necessary condition for any argument to be valid and non-fallacious. In his frequently anthologized, and even more frequently referenced article on sexist language, "'Pricks' and 'Chicks': A Plea for 'Persons'," Robert Baker demonstrates throughout that both the syntax and the semantics of English are fraught with the denigration of women.[12] He then concludes that sexual discrimination permeates the conceptual structures of our thinking. This is hardly surprising, since this is where his argument begins.

One of the most common mistakes made in moral argumentation is to attempt to deduce an "ought" from an "is" or a value judgment from a

Robert G. Pielke

factual judgment. While factual information is essential, it can not possibly provide moral support.

Justice Thurgood Marshall's dissenting opinion in *Gregg v. Georgia*, in which he argues for the unconstitutionality of the death penalty, he commits just such an error in reasoning.[13] One of his main contentions is that if the American people were fully informed as to the purposes and liabilities of the death penalty, they would find it morally objectionable. So far, there is nothing wrong with his reasoning; it is merely a conditional proposition. Yet he goes on to utilize this as a fundamental reason for finding the death penalty to be immoral. This simply does not follow, for it is obviously possible to find the death penalty moral or immoral regardless of what the American people think.

Arguably the most devastating observation that can be made about a person's argument is that it is self-contradictory — that it includes two statements, both of which can not possibly be true, thus violating the precept against non-contradiction. Rarely is the contradiction obvious; more often it involves the implications that follow from apparently compatible ideas.

Such is the case in Christopher Morris' defense of nuclear deterrence.[14] Wanting to maintain that deterrence is morally permissible in order to prevent nuclear war, he tries to have his proverbial cake while eating it. He maintains both that nuclear war would violate the absolute prohibition on directly killing innocent persons and is therefore morally wrong, and that nuclear warfare would not be immoral in a state of nature where morality does not exist. This logical contortion, however, conceals a fundamental contradiction, for deterrence is the issue — not morality. It can be granted that without morality *per se* everything would be possible, yet absent this condition the question of deterrence arises. Morris argues that while it would never be moral to use nuclear weapons, it would not be immoral to keep them around should their use become not immoral. This means that while there can be no reason to stockpile such weapons, they may indeed be stockpiled. This simply makes no sense.

One particularly insidious form or argumentation involves an appeal to something that seems to be relevant, but which is actually quite irrelevant. The various types of *ad hominem* fallacies are only the most obvious cases in point. Of greater difficulty to detect is an attempt to "poison the well." An irrelevancy of this type will attempt to structure the argument in such a way as to render any contrary claim misguided from the start.

Critiquing Moral Arguments

An unusually interesting example of such a maneuver is when Charles Keating (yes, that Charles Keating) proclaims the corrupting effects of pornography (or anything erotic). He quite openly asserts that no matter how many experts are cited or studies conducted, the evils of selling sexually explicit material for pure pleasure should be within the common sense of everyone.[15] Although he does not go on to state the obvious conclusion, it follows inexorably that all contrary opinions are illogical. (It may have been noted, in addition, that the parenthetical expression earlier in this paragraph constitutes yet another example of this same fallacy!)

So as not to overemphasize the role that both formal and informal logic play in the critical process, this one final example will have to do. It concerns the fundamental criterion for assessing the validity of an argument, namely, that it must never be possible for all the premises to be true while the conclusion is false. If so, the argument is invalid because of its structure.

Although this is always debatable in terms of actual arguments, it is nevertheless legitimately arguable about Raymond Belliotti's advocacy of a very "liberal" sexual ethic.[16] He begins with the Kantian principle to the effect that it is morally wrong to treat someone merely as means to someone's personal ends alone. This seems as justifiable as any moral claim could possibly be. He follows with another seemingly unquestionable moral principle: the notion that all proper sexual interactions are contractual, with reciprocity as its essential component. Two corollaries, given that all things are equal, are that contracts ought to be kept and promises not be broken seem; both of which seem axiomatically implicit. Thus, he alleges, sex is immoral if and only if it involves deception, promise-breaking, or the use of another as merely means to one's own ends. But surely, there are at least some uncontroversial instances wherein all the requisite conditions have been met and the sexual act is still immoral. Citing only one would be sufficient to raise serious questions about the argument. One example would be a voluntary, contractual agreement between a student and a teacher that a certain grade will be exchanged for sexual favors. It could be reasonably argued that while this meets all of his conditions, it is still immoral.

Ethical Theory

It has to be assumed that a critic will be sufficiently well-acquainted with the intricacies of normative reasoning. If not, there is no way for a

Robert G. Pielke

criticism to be complete. For the various kinds of normative moral reasoning each have their intrinsic strengths and their unavoidable weaknesses. See, for example, William Frankena's *Ethics* for an excellent survey.

Utilitarians, for example, must necessarily speculate about the balance of good over evil that would result from the adoption of a particular act, rule, or character trait. In so doing, qualities must be quantified — an inherently impossible task. Any attempt to do so will seem patently absurd if not properly qualified.

Garrett Hardin uses the clearly measurable commodity of human lives to argue that wealthy countries do not have a moral obligation to help those nations in need. While it is no doubt possible to quantify human lives, there is no way he can make intelligible the notion that the "good" to be maximized means exactly "number of lives." For he obviously assumes that not all human lives are intrinsically equal in value — at face value, a question-begging proposition that he never begins to explain or justify. Any attempt to do so, of course, would add a qualitative factor, and would merely proclaim that this is what "good" ought to mean. Furthermore, a careful reading of his argument would show that the "good" is never really identified at all, and there is no way a utilitarian argument can make sense without such a clarification.

Another inherent dilemma faced by utilitarians is whether to give greater significance to the immediate or the long term consequences in performing the utilitarian calculations. There is no way to answer this question without already knowing the answer, since the question concerns the intelligibility of the utilitarian principle itself. (For in a strictly logical sense, only a utilitarian explanation can be given as to how the principle should be utilized.)

G. L. Simons' contention that pornography is beneficial does include the acceptable suggestion that "good" means "pleasure," but he completely ignores the issue as to whether a greater pleasure for "the moment" might outweigh the pleasure likely to occur over the long run. Conceivably, the pleasure gained over time might show pornography to be undesirable, even though it might be quite pleasurable for the moment. It is not merely the idea that he fails to consider this possibility; it is the fact that, due to the structure of his reasoning, can not do so.

One final weakness inherent to utilitarian thinking is its notion that one's duty is in every instance to maximize the good. Since there is probably always something to be done that is likely to produce more good over evil on balance than any other available alternative, there can be no role for actions that are permissible; hence, no "rights!" The moral action is thus necessarily an obligation.

Consider Peter Singer's advocacy of supererogatory actions in feeding the needy. He really can do nothing else — to make maximization the basic moral obligation is to render completely unintelligible the notions of charity and moral choice. He does admit these dilemmas, but the real question is whether or not he can make sense of this approach to helping the needy.

Deontologists are in no better shape. Their problems are also inherent and equally severe. For one thing, their basic moral principles are bound to seem either absurdly general or arbitrarily specific.

Consider R. M. Hare's "Abortion and the Golden Rule."[17] His desire to establish a presumption against abortion (while permitting a veritable wealth of exceptions), is predicated entirely on this extraordinarily vague precept. Further, he admits that the "golden rule" is for all practical purposes identical to the Kantian principle of universalizability, which has itself been critiqued far and wide for providing no specific moral guidance.

The reverse is the case with Burton Leiser. In his book *Liberty, Justice and Morals*, he favors the death penalty for certain very specific crimes.[18] Granted that he makes an attempt to derive these judgments from the general guideline of retribution, there is no way that this allows him to make a distinction between killing in the heat of passion (for which the death penalty would be inappropriate) and kidnapping (for which it would be appropriate). These are his conclusions, yet they function as basic precepts — resulting in a seemingly arbitrary moral position. After all, would it not make just as much sense to make the reverse judgments about these particular crimes? (What sense does it make, for example, to threaten a kidnapper with death when the prime witness is under the perpetrator's control? The kidnapper has nothing to lose, and everything to gain, by killing the victim!)

Another structural weakness endemic to deontology is the necessity to clarify the relationship between the basic rules. This usually necessitates the introduction of yet more rules. Even if the resulting proliferation of rules can be avoided, there is no way all the possible ramifications can be dealt with so as to make this kind of moral reasoning workable.

John Finnis, in *Natural Law and Unnatural Acts*, appeals to natural law in his opposition to such allegedly questionable behavior as homosexuality and masturbation.[19] In so doing he makes reference to

Robert G. Pielke

various "basic goods" and "virtues," but how such values as "procreation" and the "unitive significance" of intercourse are related is never clarified sufficiently. Many explanatory principles are introduced — too many to follow. Finally, there is an intelligibility problem whenever deontologists refer to their basic principles. It derives from something like the following enigma: If the amount of value associated with or produced by an action or rule is not relevant to its moral evaluation, what is? The attempts to respond have always raised more questions than they have answered. Kant cited "Reason." Marx cited "History." Cicero cited "Nature." Rousseau cited "the General Will." Augustine cited "God." Herbert Spencer cited "Darwin." These are among the most successful in their attempts to clarify the basic principles of morality.

Mortimer and Sanford Kadish argue that there are legally justifiable departures from the legal rules within an officially sanctioned organization. Their *Official Disobedience* is a lengthy series of arguments to show just how this apparent contradiction isn't.[20] Their tortured reasoning stems in large part from their reliance on the Kantian maxim to treat others as autonomous and free beings. As stated the maxim can direct a person to protest unfair practices in an institution that is fully justified — but protest in such a way as to question the institution's justifiability. "Autonomy" and "freedom" are notoriously slippery concepts, and in their argument it is fundamentally unclear what meaning they can possibly have.

Those who make use of Classical moral reasoning, relying primarily on the inculcation of virtues and the avoidance of vices, fall prey to a variety of problems. One of the major difficulties is being able to determine whether a person has the requisite set of virtues (and has escaped having the most serious vices). No matter how clearly they are specified, there must always remain a greater or lesser degree of uncertainty as to whether a person is really acting morally or immorally.

Daniel Callahan would freely grant a woman the right to choose an abortion — as long as her decision is made with the greatest of seriousness.[21] She must, among other things, have a great respect for human life. But how is someone to determine whether she has met this as well as the other conditions? Callahan cannot reply, since motivations are internal — and intrinsically beyond the reach of empirical scrutiny. There is thus no way intelligibly to implement his ethical notions.

Another serious problem, making Classical moral reasoning still more questionable, is its inability to distinguish those character traits that are morally relevant from those that are not. Even the Classical virtues of wisdom, prudence, courage, and temperance are question-begging. Not only is it unclear what they mean, it is not immediately convincing why they are supposedly moral qualities. Even the remaining virtue, courage, is easily doubted as an obligatory character trait — desirable, praiseworthy, commendable, and no doubt to be encouraged — but is it so obvious that a person lacking courage is thus blameworthy?

Thomas Hill's antipathy to the trait of servility, arguing that it is a vice akin to arrogance, is only persuasive on the surface. While few would dispute that arrogant people (and perhaps servile people) are unlikable, it does not follow that they are immoral. Hill does not make the connection, and can not do so without bringing in some other moral guidelines — which he seems loath to do.

Ethical Egoism, a much maligned form of thinking (often for the wrong reasons), suffers what many believe to be one fatal weakness — obviating the necessity to find others. It concerns the logical prerequisite for any moral guideline to be universalized. (Otherwise, a prescription can only be, at best, prudential.) In so doing, however, the ethical egoist must, while encouraging all persons to adopt ethical egoism, be urging something that is highly unlikely to be in his or her best interests. Although not a logical contradiction, this would most probably lead to the most egregious kind of strife and tension in a social setting. So the description of the difficulty goes.

Every ethical egoist should be aware of this, and make some kind of attempt to devise some response. Adam Smith, for example, relied on what he called "the Invisible Hand" which in all probability was what he conceived of as the "laws of supply and demand." In any case, the critic should be very sensitive to such attempts and question whether or not they are successful.

John Hospers, in an essay entitled, "What Libertarianism Is," asserts a more explicit and more contemporary version of Adam Smith's reliance on a free market.[22] Appraising this critically does not require questioning the laws of supply and demand. This is actually beside the point. What needs to be questioned is whether this kind of answer is even relevant to the problem. Hospers must show that it is, and how so, but nowhere does he do this. The connection is not immediately obvious.

George Will takes another approach. In his analysis of attempts to secure aid for the needy — the handicapped in particular — he prefers to rely on the sense of benevolence both individually and legislatively.[23] To put it another way (a tactic which the critic should develop), Will is saying that the kind of conflict feared by non-ethical egoists can be avoided. He is not claiming that encouraging benevolence would be easy — quite the contrary. The critic, however, should go beyond simply disputing his still confident assessment of the community's potential. The critic should wonder whether any degree of confidence would be satisfactory. Again, how does this relate to the problem at hand? Will does not say.

Basic Assumptions

Basic assumptions can not be legitimately challenged in a critique, no matter how much the critic may disagree with them. Rather, the focus must be on whether or not the moral conclusions are consistent with the assumptions being held.

A frequently overlooked facet of moral reasoning, yet one of paramount significance, concerns the assumptions a person makes regarding human nature. There are two kinds. One relates to whether humans are, by nature, social (the root meaning for "socialism") or individualistic ("individualism"). Depending upon which assumption is held, the possible kinds of social institutions will vary. In general, one will lead to a socialist economic arrangement of some kind; while the other will imply a market economy in one form or another.

Ronald Duska contends that "whistle blowing" raises no significant moral dilemmas, since individuals owe no duties to profit-making organizations. In his *Whistleblowing and Employee Loyalty*[24], he argues that the capitalist corporate structures are incompatible with human nature. Yet as someone who seems to be an advocate of the individualistic assumption, this assertion of incompatibility is questionable.

The same tension, although in reverse, is evident in the position of Jeffrie Murphy in *Marxism and Retribution*.[25] He opposes capital punishment because of its incompatibility with human nature, but his rejection of the individualistic assumption does not clearly entail this opposition. He merely asserts this implication without explanation.

The other type of assumption regarding human nature relates to the degree of confidence a person has about humans being able to behave morally — without external guidance or pressure. Of necessity, a given assumption will fall somewhere on a continuum, with some persons more or less pessimistic and others more or less optimistic.

Critiquing Moral Arguments

Returning to the article by George Will, his reliance on benevolence clearly depends on a relatively optimistic view about humanity. If this is the case, he would seemingly have little use for a legislative approach, an approach that quite consciously does not rely too heavily on voluntarism. This tension is not necessarily fatal, but it does require far more in the way of an explanation than he provides.

On the other hand, Gregory Kavka's defense of nuclear deterrence, his article previously mentioned, is supported by a relatively pessimistic outlook. He makes the connection between his assumption and deterrence to be one of necessity, the strongest kind of claim. Yet this necessary entailment is never even acknowledged, much less explained and defended.

Another key assumption having a crucial impact on moral reasoning is similarly metaphysical, but it extends to far more than human nature. It concerns the question of "determinism." If human choice is not determined by heredity, environment, or anything else, then every person bears some degree of moral responsibility for his or her actions. If, on the other hand, all human choices are completely explainable (theoretically if not actually) in terms of prior events, then the question of moral responsibility has to be understood quite differently.

Marxists, like Jeffrie Murphy, referred to earlier, will usually maintain that criminal behavior results from the social conditions created by capitalism. Hence punishment, the justifiable infliction of harms, would seem to be illicit under any and all circumstances. Yet this does not necessarily follow. A utilitarian (i.e., a deterrence) account would seem to be an equally possible alternative. Strictly speaking, guilt or innocence is not relevant for the utilitarian position on punishment — the achievement of deterrence is the sole consideration.

For a retributivist like Burton Leiser, the same kind of difficulty exists. Obviously in favor of the institution of punishment, it would seem to be vital for him to affirm the freedom of an individual's choice from deterministic pressures. Yet he suggests numerous instances when capital punishment ought not to be used because the criminal act results from environmental and/or psychological causes. Again, there is nothing logically suspicious about noting exceptions of this kind. Indeed, it would be remiss of him not to do so. The problem is that he never addresses the question of delineating between excusable and inexcusable situations. He obviously has such a line in mind, but he never clarifies where it is and how it is drawn. Hence, the critic might suggest that his excusing conditions are determined arbitrarily.

Robert G. Pielke

The Burden of Proof

One of the most overlooked facets of doing a critique of a moral argument is making note of who has the burden of proof. Since moral reasoning is <u>always</u> concerned with, at the very least, the prevention of harm, any action or character trait that could <u>possibly</u> lead to the rightful infliction of harm must be defended. To put it negatively, any action or character trait that does not involve the possibility of harm does not require any defense at all. Obviously, then, any action or trait that would <u>necessarily</u> lead to harm has without question the strongest possible burden of proof.

These distinctions are crucial in performing a critique. For example, it is probably non-controversial that execution is more harmful than life in prison. This being the case, the burden of proof falls on those who advocate capital punishment. On the opposite extreme, it is no less unproblematic that sexual intercourse between two voluntarily consenting adults is morally permissible. Hence, it is incumbent on those who feel such actions are wrong to provide a defense. When the issues are so patently clear, rarely are the mistakes in reasoning obvious.

Of course it could happen that someone will <u>try</u> to place the burden of proof on his or her opponent, but such flaws are easily identified and demolished. For example, the encyclical forbidding to Roman Catholics any artificial means of birth control attempts to cite the harm consequent to such action.[26] The "harm" turns out to be a violation of "god's will" — a "sin" perhaps, but not a harm. At best, the only claim that can be made here is that there is a religious, not a moral, obligation. Permitting artificial means of birth control does not require any defense; the restriction of such means has the burden of proof. Similarly, the Massachusetts Appeals Court decided to allow doctors to withdraw all life-support machinery from a patient who could no longer benefit from such measures.[27] There was no need to defend this action; the only potential for harm was to continue the useless measures. The burden of proof was on those who opposed the withdrawal.

More often than not, mistakes in reasoning concern the large middle ground where there exists the <u>possibility</u> of harm. These are the more problematic instances when it is not clear whether harm is a factor or not. In such cases, questions such as, What constitutes 'harm'?, Is harm to the self alone relevant?, and, Is it possible to harm 'society'? inevitably arise. If questions of this kind are not adequately addressed, there is the basis for a significant critique. For as a result of such omissions, the issue of who has the burden of proof is necessarily begged.

G. L. Simons claims that not only is pornography unharmful but that it is beneficial in his article mentioned earlier entitled "Is Pornography Beneficial?" His support for this contention is essentially that no proof exists that it is harmful (the fallacy of "negative proof"), and that it may have a cathartic effect. His attempt is essentially to shift the burden of proof to those who would censor this kind of material. It is certainly a worthy tactic, but it could be argued that his attempt is woefully insufficient.

In one of the most influential court cases in the state of California, it was decided that the plaintiff, a woman teacher named Pettit, rightfully had her elementary school teaching credential revoked by the state.[28] The reason cited was moral turpitude; her behavior at a private sex club would make it impossible for her to act as a moral example. Yet very little evidence, if any, was cited to support this contention. The argument made for the majority by Justice Burke contended that the burden of proof was on Pettit to show that her actions constituted no possible harm. This, however, misplaces the burden of proof, since there is no obvious connection between her private behavior and her role as a moral example.

While it might be conceded that harm is the primary factor in establishing the burden of proof, there is another to keep in mind — the relevance of the harm. Christopher Stone's controversial monograph "Should Trees Have Standing?" fails in this sense.[29] There is no question that cutting down trees and destroying natural objects is harmful — but is the harm done of any moral significance? The burden of proof is clearly on Stone, yet he never successfully makes sense of his claim. Note that if he were to have done so, the burden of proof would clearly shift to those who want to cut down trees!

A variation on this theme is to claim that while relevant harm might result from a given action, the harm is nevertheless justifiable. Richard Wasserstrom, in "Preferential Treatment," contends that the arguments against affirmative action programs are ineffective since they inflict no unjust harm on persons being denied jobs.[30] As with the arguments just mentioned, his tactic is to shift the burden of proof. If he is successful, the onus of proof, so he thinks, is no longer on him. In making this attempt, he raises questions about "qualifications" and whether or not it makes sense to say that we deserve rewards because we possess them. This is beside the point. It makes very little difference, logically, whether we do or do not

Robert G. Pielke

deserve our qualifications. Harm is almost certainly the consequence for those not hired because of such programs. Wasserstrom can not avoid shouldering the burden of proof by this method. If he could, those against affirmative action programs would have the burden, and this is simply nonsense.

The Fundamental Issue

Another, even more frequently overlooked facet of moral reasoning subject to critical scrutiny concerns the identity of the fundamental issue. Underlying every genuine moral dilemma is some irreducible conflict that, if not properly understood, will involve a faulty analysis of the problem, and the argument will seem more or less beside the point.

The abortion controversy, for example, is predicated on a metaphysical dispute between Realists and Nominalists; the dispute over punishment reduces to assumptions regarding the causes of crime; euthanasia boils down to essentially legal questions; and sexism grows out of beliefs about whether sex roles are innate or learned.

An egregious example of how this kind of omission can make an argument seem ridiculous is the Bandman's efforts to arrive at moral guidelines concerning euthanasia. Since they truly seem completely unaware that the real problems are legal, none of their examples are to the point. Either they cite problems that have nothing to do with euthanasia, or they waste time dealing with obviously resolvable, pseudo-dilemmas. Not once do they mention the legal facet of the issue.

Justice Rehnquist, writing the majority opinion for the United States Supreme Court in *Rostker v. Goldberg*, in which the question was whether or not women should be registered for the draft, never even alludes to the nature of sex roles.[31] While he clearly represents a point of view which believes sex roles to be innate and not learned, this does not form any part of his argument. As a consequence, the majority's opinion that women ought not to be required to register seems completely arbitrary.

Another legal opinion, in this case Sandra Day O'Connor's dissenting opinion in an abortion case immediately after her ascending to the Supreme Court, can be critiqued for essentially the same reason. *Akron v. Akron Center for Reproductive Health* concerned some rather obvious attempts to make it difficult for a woman to choose an abortion.[32] The court struck down the laws in question, but O'Connor felt that *Roe v. Wade's* use of the trimester division of pregnancy was a poor way to decide the compelling point when the state might intervene. She went on to argue that "viability" is relative to whatever state of technology happens to be current. Although she is certainly correct, this is entirely irrelevant as far as her opposition to the majority's opinion is concerned. She wants to maintain, and clearly writes, that the potentiality of a fetus' humanity exists from the moment of conception. Thus the state's interest begins at conception. This is an argument based on the position of a metaphysical Realist — a fact that she never acknowledges. This makes her argument about viability strangely irrelevant, since she ostensibly relies so heavily on it.

Regarding the issue of punishment, and its seemingly far more controversial corollary — capital punishment — Sidney Hook's "The Death Sentence" takes a peculiar position.[33] He contends, as a supposed defender of the death penalty, that it should be limited to those who murder twice and those who request it! These two exceptions should immediately raise certain questions about the kind of persons he would subject to execution. It would seem only fair to wonder, for example, whether anyone who requested execution was completely sane. Someone who is likely to repeatedly murder would also seem to be mentally questionable. Even if most of them turn out to be completely sane, the more fundamental issue as to the causes of their actions should arise. Why is it, after all, that some people kill others and others do not? Hook never alludes to this basic concern, and so his argument seems to be missing something — it is: the fundamental issue.

The analysis of a moral problem must always include some awareness of the underlying source of the dilemma. It need not be the primary focus of the argument, but the argument must be informed by it, and this awareness should be in evidence. This should not suggest, however, that there is unanimity concerning the identity of fundamental issues. As with most matters at issue, there is more or less agreement. The disputes just identified are generally agreed upon as fundamental, but there are others that are as ferociously debated as the moral issue itself. The point is that a moral argument must make a genuine attempt to relate the specific problem to its broader context and deeper source.

Factual Support

Although the conclusion of a moral argument, by definition, can never be a factual observation, inevitably there will be factual information provided as support. There are several ways to question this material

Robert G. Pielke

critically, and in each case it must be made clear why the factual problem is relevant.

One very obvious way is to wonder about the accuracy of the support. Unless the critic is evaluating a historically dated moral argument, it is unlikely that any really blatant inaccuracies will be found. Moral thinkers are not attempting to dispute what is; they are making use of accepted empirical data to dispute what ought to be. Nevertheless, it sometimes happens that more subtle errors will be relied upon. In Helen Longino's "Pornography, Oppression, and Freedom: A Closer Look," she makes a strong case for censorship.[34] In so doing, however, she depends on the material in question being essentially about the abusive and degrading portrayal of women. Her whole argument for censorship largely depends on the truth of this implicit claim. Yet, in fact, there is as much pornographic material about men — exclusively about men — as about women. This weakens her case considerably.

Another consideration is to wonder about omissions of significant information — intentional or otherwise. This is a far more common flaw in the use of factual material — and often difficult to detect, since the critic would be noting an absence, the non-presence of something that should be there. Alison Jaggar's ostensibly descriptive account of "Political Philosophies of Women's Liberation," is a case in point.[35] This, despite the fact that she qualifies what she is doing by saying that she is only going to deal with those philosophical positions that are the most influential. She describes five, but nowhere does she even mention the feminist movements within organized religion. Both the numbers of women involved and the amount of writing in the area would seem to make them clearly as influential as any of the others — and more so than most.

A third way to question the factual support is to point out that the information cited is irrelevant — or not as relevant as it should be. Justice Marshall's opposition to the death penalty is based partly on what he believes to be American public opinion, if it were ever to be fully informed. Granted that his use of the subjunctive immunizes the claim from being false, it is nevertheless completely irrelevant. Even if one hundred percent of the American people were to oppose the death penalty, this would not make it immoral. It is simply not possible to derive a moral conclusion from a factual assertion — no matter how unquestionable the factual assertion might be.

Finally, the critic should be as sensitive as possible to the fact that facts are always presented in an interpretive scheme. There is no such thing as "raw data." This is because an interpretation is what gives <u>meaning</u> to the data — thus producing "information." There is no other way data can be utilized. In the presentation (or interpretation) of data, however, there might also be presented what could generously be called "wishful thinking." For example, in Douglas Lackey's utilitarian proposal for unilateral nuclear disarmament, he cites (among other things) the "fact" that the atomic bombing of Hiroshima and Nagasaki had almost no effect on Japan's decision to surrender. Hence, the strategic effect of such weapons can be seriously questioned. The claim that this bombing had no effect, however, is highly interpretive and certainly debatable. He is aware that his belief runs counter to conventional wisdom, and thus he supports it with still more debatable notions. Now, it might very well be the case that his interpretation is correct. But it <u>is</u> an interpretation, and not a claim subject to empirical scrutiny.

Describing the Action

Rarely is critical attention directed toward one of the more subtly problematic aspects of moral argumentation — describing the action. The physical movements of the body are only one component, and often not the most significant. There are at least two others worth considering: the intentions and the consequences.

The critic's job is to determine which of the three are appropriate to include in the argument. The problem is that the very moral judgment sought in the conclusion might in effect be "begged" by incorporating it into a description of the action. The most obvious example of this is "euthanasia," literally a "happy death." So when debating the "happy death," the arguments are in effect mostly about the desirability of this particular kind of consequence. There is absolutely no mention made of how this end might be accomplished, but it really does not matter. The goal is the crucial thing — hardly controversial when understood literally.

Debating "nuclear deterrence," when properly analyzed, is actually a debate over intentions. (Remember, deterrence can never be measured. Logically, measurement would entail the observation of "non-events." Hence, the only meaning it can have is the kind of result <u>sought</u>, i.e., intended.) The only action involved is the "stockpiling" of nuclear weapons. So the action as well as the actual consequences are, accordingly, de-emphasized when considering this particular issue. Of course, these latter ingredients are precisely what matters — not the intention. (Everyone wants to deter nuclear war!)

When arguing about the action described as "censorship," there is no stress given to either the intentions or the actual consequences — exactly those factors that are problematic. Few would argue for the desirability of censorship *per se*.

The critic's responsibility is to note whether there is any subtle reliance on the unproblematic facts of the action at issue to make the case. Although tactically astute, this is illicit. (It would constitute "begging the question" in some sense.) Rarely will a moral thinker utilize this tactic to the exclusion of anything else, but it often forms a part of an argument. Yet even the smallest reliance on this kind of device should be rejected as inappropriate.

George Sher preys upon the unproblematically negative connotations of "reverse discrimination" in his "Justifying Reverse Discrimination in Employment" in order to oppose it.[36] While he certainly gives some attention to both the specific institutional "movements" involved in such programs as well as their consequences, he tends to rely more than a little on the undesirable intentions. This makes his task far easier than it might otherwise be.

In arguing for the desirability of aiding the needy, Alan Gewirth emphasizes the unproblematically negative connotations of the physical condition indicated by the term "starvation."[37] This is not entirely fair. Greater attention should be given to both the motives for giving aid as well as the consequences of doing so. A full consideration of aiding needy would have to look dispassionately beyond the spirit-crushing reality of people starving to death.

The unproblematically desirable consequences are stressed in John Passmore's *Conservation and Posterity*.[38] The term "conservation" refers primarily to the effects of a series of actions. By doing so, specific enactments required to bring about this result and the underlying motivations for doing so are de-emphasized. Relying on the positive connotations of an unquestionably positive idea, a tactical advantage is introduced without the necessity of a reasoned defense.

Cases

The most concrete part of a moral argument is often the citation of cases pertinent to the issue. As noted in Chapter Two, sometimes these cases are used merely to illustrate a point. At other times they form the core of the argument itself. It is this latter situation that provides the critic with a possible opportunity for attack. While attacking an illustration may be satisfying psychologically, it has little critical impact. The typical response is simply to substitute another example for one that is flawed. Attacking a facet of the argument, however, will force the person making the argument to reformulate or perhaps even abandon the original position.

What is difficult in determining in which category a given case most appropriately fits. It is rarely clear. Many times a particular case will function in both ways. To be safe, the critic might just as well evaluate more ways than fewer — always being sure to point out why the failure in this instance is damaging to the argument as a whole.

Another distinction worth keeping in mind is the fact that some cases are actual instances and others are hypothetical constructions. Although this may at first glance seem very significant, it is less so when properly understood. Admittedly, a hypothetical case can be constructed in just such a way as to enable the argument to succeed when it might otherwise fail. So also might an actual instance perform this function; for no matter how detailed an actual case is presented, there will always be an element of interpretation and selectivity. The inevitable temptation will thus be to interpret and select in such a way as to make the argument succeed. For either type of case, it is incumbent on the critic to point out how this is being done.

One of the most absurd attempts to construct a case just to make a point is in Michael Levin's "The Case for Torture."[39] His contention is that torture in some cases is not only morally permissible, it is mandatory — in order to prevent future or greater evils. This utilitarian form of argument only works if there is some kind of empirical support — a reasonable speculation to the effect that more lives can on occasion be saved by torture than would be the case without torture. To show this, he constructs a scenario wherein someone has planted a bomb on an airplane, a bomb that only the terrorist can disarm, and (note carefully) only by torture! It is left aside for the moment the absurdity that the terrorist is on the ground (!) — making even remorseful cooperation irrelevant. Levin has described the situation in such a way that presupposes the very conclusion he is seeking to establish. This hardly establishes his contention.

Bertram and Elsie Bandman construct four hypothetical cases that supposedly only illustrate their theoretical distinctions regarding when euthanasia is permissible and when it is not. It is strange that none of the four seem even vaguely relevant to their guidelines. In one case, like Levin's just mentioned, a doctor does not have the right to die since he alone possesses knowledge of how to cure a disease that will extinguish life in his community. His own desire to avoid a painful death from cancer must be postponed. A second case involves the illicit desire of a family to rid itself of someone who is a drain on their finances. This would be murder! The third presents the dilemma of a mother who must consider donating a kidney to one of two sons who need it. This is a case of self-sacrifice! The final case is about a person who is in the terminal stages of dying and nothing can be done to extend the dying process. This does not present any kind of dilemma at all — much less a moral dilemma!

In their desire to show how their principles can operate in real life, they have actually does the opposite. If not one single instance can be created to make their point, considerable doubt is raised about the intelligibility of their theory.

As with most judicial decisions, the citation of similar cases from the past forms a crucial part of the argument. These are, of course, actual cases. Still, there is no intrinsic protection from mistakes in relying on actual situations. Real life is not self-interpreting. Consider the *Pettit v. State Board of Education* mentioned earlier. The principle appealed to was the notion that no one could be barred from a profession on grounds unrelated to the performance of professional duties. In supporting Pettit's removal for moral turpitude, the majority contended that allegedly similar instances in the past were actually not as similar as they might appear. Although moral turpitude was common to all the cited cases, Pettit's conduct involved the possibility of harm. Even if Pettit's actions did involve the possibility of harm (which seems doubtful to the minority), the other cases were described so as to de-emphasize any possibility of harm. The selective description is crucial. Similarity or dissimilarity is thereby established for the sake of the argument.

Analogies

Analogies function in the same way as cases, having both illustrative and logical roles to play. Also, they can be both actual or hypothetical. With reference to analogies, however, there is an additional factor to keep in mind: for an analogy to work, there must be (1) a sufficient number of (2) relevant similarities. An argument using analogies can be critiqued not only for the same reasons a case-based argument can be critiqued, it can be critiqued for these other reasons as well.

Charles Keating's opposition to pornography is partially based on what he feels are its inevitably bad consequences. In order to make this claim stick, he cites the allegedly similar instance of the moral decay having destroyed most of the world's great civilizations. This is a reference to actual, allegedly similar situations — pornography implicitly analogized with moral decay. His brief reference, however, conceals the vast amount of characteristics differentiating these civilizations. It further obscures the fact that many of these characteristics, even if similar, may not be relevant. The critic should cite a few to make the point.

Gregory Kavka creates a very brief analogy to demonstrate his belief that unilateral nuclear disarmament would be insane. He asks the reader to imagine what a bank robber would do upon learning the bank had done away with locks and guards. While rhetorically quite effective, it is possible to raise many questions regarding the number of similarities and their relevance. Are two similarities (weapons and an aggressor) at all sufficient? Further, are bank robbers and nations in any way relevantly similar?

Perhaps the most infamous use of hypothetical analogies is undertaken by Judith Jarvis Thomson in her much anthologized "A Defense of Abortion."[40] In order to argue that abortions can be deemed permissible even by those who regard the fetus as fully human from the moment of conception, she shows that it would be quite appropriate to disconnect a famous violinist from your kidneys when the violinist had been attached against your will. She is careful to limit this analogy to cases of rape, and so avoids the obvious criticism that women often decide to have an abortion for convenience. Yet her analogy, while it does portray a forcible connection of a dependent person onto you, it nevertheless ignores the massive dissimilarity between a microscopic "person" and one fully grown. The mobility factor alone would make attachment to the violinist a far different matter.

Another of her inventions concerns contraception analogized with window screens to keep out undesirable "people seeds," which might, if allowed, grow in your rugs and furniture. While the similarity is obvious , and humorous, there is a striking difference between people growing inside you and people growing in something like test tubes!

Her last analogy is a real one between a woman being asked to carry a child and the self-giving actions of a "good," a "minimally decent," and a "splendid" Samaritan. At this point, none of the alleged similarities are defensible, for she is attempting to analogize a moral dilemma with supererogatory concerns. The two are incommensurate forms of thinking, and thus it is inherently faulty.

CONCLUSION

This small manual is intended as an introduction to the art of the critique — and it cannot be stressed enough that critiquing is most definitely an art. Far from being a mere mechanical procedure, it requires sensitivity, insight, equanimity, and, above all, practice. Even then, there is no guarantee that a critique will be immune to response. On the contrary, if a critic has done a good job, a response is virtually certain to follow. It is often true that the better the critique, the more vociferous the response. A poor critique can be safely ignored — not being worth the effort to respond. So while there is no sure fire way to evaluate the success of a critique, the critic can be assured that his or her comments have hit home if a counter attack is launched.

This raises an important point that should be kept in mind. No matter how devastating the critique may seem — to the critic, a critique is never self-authenticating. It will always require a defense. The critic's task is not finished, in other words, when the allegations are made. All the possible responses should be anticipated and taken fully into account. Even then, the task is still not finished. For in a very real sense, it is never finished. Any provocative book or article can (and should) engender endless debate. This is the very stuff of moral disputation. After all, if genuine moral dilemmas are at issue, continuing disputes can not be avoided. Such disputes are not capable of easy resolution — or any resolution in most cases. The best that can be hoped for is clarity, and possibly respect. When the disagreements are particularly virulent, respect might even be anathema to the contending parties. So be it.

This brings up yet another reminder. Critiquing a moral argument is not, and should not, be a game. A critique is to a moral argument as a logical analysis is to the reasoning process in general. It is not akin to "debating," which _is_ a game — having its own set of objectives and rules. When attacking the fervently held positions of others (even if these very same positions held by the critic), the conceptual tools are not toys; they are weapons.

One final thought to keep in mind concerns the implicit seriousness of what has just been said. Philosophy, as often alleged, does not enable a person to critique moral arguments simply for the sake of doing so. Not everything can be attacked or defended from a philosophical perspective — nor should it. No philosophical thinker worthy of this inherently ambiguous label would ever deem it acceptable to defend the reinstitution of slavery, or attack the supposition that killing innocent persons is always morally suspect. To critique for the sake of critiquing, as with arguing for the sake of arguing, is a fundamentally worthless activity.

Perhaps it all comes down to this: If a moral position is worth having, it is worth critiquing.

Notes

1. Mary Anne Warren, "On the Moral and Legal Status of Abortion" in THE MONIST, Vol. 57, No. 1 (January 1973); Jane English, "Abortion and the Concept of a Person" in CANADIAN JOURNAL OF PHILOSOPHY, Vol. 5, No. 2 (October 1975).

2. Peter Singer, "Famine, Affluence, and Morality" in PHILOSOPHY & PUBLIC AFFAIRS 1, No. 3 (Spring 1972); Garrett Hardin, "Living on a Lifeboat" in BIOSCIENCE, October 1974.

3. D. H. M. Brooks, "Why Discrimination is Especially Wrong" in JOURNAL OF VALUE INQUIRY, Vol. 17 (1983); Michael E. Levin, "Is Racial Discrimination Special?" in JOURNAL OF VALUE INQUIRY, Vol. 15 (1981).

4. Douglas Lackey, "Missiles and Morals: A Utilitarian Look at Nuclear Deterrence" in PHILOSOPHY & PUBLIC AFFAIRS 11, No. 3 (Summer 1982); Gregory Kavka, "Doubts about Unilateral Nuclear Disarmament" in PHILOSOPHY & PUBLIC AFFAIRS 12, No. 3 (Summer 1983).

5. Albert Carr, "Is Business Bluffing Ethical?" in THE HARVARD BUSINESS REVIEW, 46:1 (January-February 1968).

6. G. L. Simons, "Is Pornography Beneficial?" from Pornography Without Prejudice (London: Abelard-Schuman, 1972).

7. United States Supreme Court. 438 U.S. 265 (1978)

8. J. Gay-Williams, "The Wrongfulness of Euthanasia" in Intervention and Reflection: Basic Issues in Medical Ethics (Belmont, California: Wadsworth, 1979).

9. Thomas E. Hill, Jr., "Servility and Self-Respect" in THE MONIST, Vol. 57, No. 1 (January 1973).

10. Bertram and Elsie Bandman, "Rights, Justice and Euthanasia" in Beneficient Euthanasia, ed. by Marvin Kohl (Buffalo, New York: Prometheus Books, 1975).

11. Lisa Newton, "Reverse Discrimination As Unjustified" in ETHICS, 83:4 (1973).

12. Robert Baker, "'Pricks' and 'Chicks': A Plea for Persons" in Philosophy & Sex, ed. by Baker and Elliston (New York: Prometheus Books, 1975).

13. United States Supreme Court. 428 U.S. 153 (1976).

14. Christopher Morris, "The Ethics of Nuclear Deterrence: A Contractarian Account" in Ethics: Theory and Practice, ed. by Velasquez and Rostankowski (Englewood Cliffs, New Jersey: Prentice Hall, 1985).

15. Charles Keating, THE REPORT OF THE COMMISSION ON OBSCENITY AND PORNOGRAPHY (Washington, D. C.: Government Printing Office, 1970).

16. Raymond Belliotti, "A Philosophical Analysis of Sexual Ethics" in JOURNAL OF SOCIAL PHILOSOPHY, Vol. 10, No. 3 (September 1979).

17. R. M. Hare, "Abortion and the Golden Rule" in PHILOSOPHY & PUBLIC AFFAIRS, Vol. 4, No. 3 (Spring 1975).

18. Burton Leiser, Liberty, Justice and Morals (New York: Macmillan, 1979).

19. John Finnis, "Natural Law and Unnatural Acts" in THE HEYTHROP JOURNAL, Vol. 11, No. 4 (October 1970).

20. Mortimer & Sanford Kadish, Discretion to Disobey (California: Stanford University Press, 1973).

21. Daniel Callahan, Abortion: Law, Choice and Morality (New York: Macmillan, 1970).

22. John Hospers, "What Libertarianism" in The Libertarian Alternative, ed. by Tibor Machan.

23. George Will, "For the Handicapped: Rights But No Welcome" in THE HASTINGS CENTER REPORT 16:3 (1986).

24. Ronald Dusk, "Whistleblowing and Employee Loyalty" in Contemporary Issues in Business Ethics, ed. by Desjardins and McCall (Belmont, California: Wadsworth Publishing Company, 1985).

25. Jeffrie Murphy, "Marxism and Retribution" in PHILOSOPHY & PUBLIC AFFAIRS, Vol. 2, No. 3 (Spring 1973).

26. Pope Paul VI, "Human Vitae," July 25, 1968.

27. *Matter of Earle N. Spring*, Massachusetts Appeals Court, Adv. Sh. (1979) 2469.

28. *Pettit v. State Board of Education*, 10 C3D 29; 109 CAL. RPTR. 665, 513 P.2D 889 (1973).

29. Christopher Stone, "Should Trees Have Standing? Toward Legal Rights for Natural Objects" in SOUTHERN CALIFORNIA LAW REVIEW, 45 (1972).

30. Richard Wasserstrom, "Preferential Treatment" in Philosophy & Social Issues (Notre Dame: University of Notre Dame Press, 1980).

31. *Rostke v. Goldberg*. United States Supreme Court. 453 U.S. 57 (1981)

32. *Akron v. Center for Reproductive Health*. United States Supreme Court. 462 U.S. 416 (1983).

33. Sidney Hook, "The Death Sentence" in The Death Penalty in America, ed. by Bedau (Garden City, New York: Doubleday, 1967).

34. Helen Longino, "Pornography, Oppression, and Freedom: A Closer Look" in Take Back the Night: Women on Pornography, ed. by Lederer (New York: William Morrow, 1980).

35. Alison Jaggar, "Political Philosophies of Women's Liberation" in Today's Moral Problems, ed. by Wasserstrom (New York: Macmillan, 1985).

36. George Sher, "Justifying Reverse Discrimination in Employment" in PHILOSOPHY & PUBLIC AFFAIRS, Vol. 4, No. 2 (Spring 1975).

37. Alan Gewirth, "Starvation and Human Rights" in Ethics and Problems in the 21st Century, ed. by Goodpaster and Sayre (Norte Dame: Notre Dame Press, 1979).

38. John Passmore, Man's Responsibility for Nature (New York: Charles Scribner's Sons, 1974).

39. Michael Levin, "The Case for Torture" in NEWSWEEK, June 7, 1982.

40. Judith Jarvis Thomson, "A Defense of Abortion" in PHILOSOPHY & PUBLIC AFFAIRS, Vol. 1, No. 1 (1971).

Index